THE NEW CHINA

POSTERS

Editors-in-Chief: Chen Lyusheng, Chen Du

1950s —— 1990s

SendPoints

THE NEW CHINA

POSTERS

SendPoints

PUBLISHED BY SendPoints Publishing Co., Ltd.

EXECUTIVE EDITOR: Luo Yanmei

DESIGN DIRECTOR: Lin Shijian

EXECUTIVE ART EDITOR: Chen Ting

PROOFREADING: Weiji Li

REGISTERED ADDRESS: Room 15A Block 9 Tsui Chuk Garden, Wong Tai Sin, Kowloon, Hong Kong

TEL: +852-35832323 / **FAX:** +852-35832448

OFFICE ADDRESS: 7F, 9th Anning Street, Jinshazhou, Baiyun District, Guangzhou, China

TEL: +86-20-89095121 / **FAX:** +86-20-89095206

BEIJING OFFICE: Beijing Office: Flat 1701, Block C, BBMG International, Wangjing West Road no.48, Chaoyang District, Beijing, China

TEL: +86-10-84139071 / **FAX:** +86-10-84139071

SHANGHAI OFFICE: Shanghai Office: Room 302, Floor 3, Ningbo Road no.349, Huangpu District, Shanghai, China

TEL: +86-21-63523469 / **FAX:** +86-21-63523469

SALES MANAGER: Sissi

TEL: +86-20-81007895

EMAIL: sales@sendpoints.cn

WEBSITE: www.sendpoints.cn / www.spbooks.cn

ISBN 978-988-79283-1-7

Printed and bound in China.

THE RISE AND FALL OF THE NEW CHINA POSTERS

The Rise

The New China poster is a special product of the 20th century, with its roots in advertisements, posters and placards. While the latter mostly serves commercial purposes, the former is aimed to satisfy political and social needs.

Posters of this style appeared in the 1930s when the Second Sino-Japanese War broke out. Confined by objective conditions, they were mainly woodcut prints. The themes were about presenting fighting scenes and encouraging fighting spirit. The whole images were usually paired with agitating slogans. All in all, the artistic side of the posters was not emphasized at the time.

After the founding of New China in 1949, publicity posters were highly valued by the new government, and gradually became a popular art form among people. At the time, China began to learn almost everything from the Soviet Union, including the political system and social lifestyle. The art of poster was no exception. The publicity posters of the Soviet Union set an example for China, especially causing the rough-styled posters created from 1935 to 1948 (also known as the Yan'an period) transform into a Western style painting characteristic of fighting morale and delicate artistry.

The Prosperity

After the 1950s, promoted by political movements and influenced by the Soviet arts, the New China posters began to take shape. As most people were illiterate at that time, these posters became the best tool to educate people, raise their awareness of national unity, guide and organize people towards the same aim.

Entering the 1950s, the posters were developed to reflect national policies and political movements. As more and more painters devoted to this art form, the artistic level of the posters was improved drastically. However, the posters also had obvious shortcomings: conceptualized themes, narrow-ranged subjects, superficial understanding of subjects, formulated painting techniques, and stereotyped artistic style.

From the late 1950s and the early 1960s, the New China posters developed rapidly, and show a growing political inclination. Poster became one of the most popular art forms, for its steadily improved artistry. During this period, the posters catered closely to the political tasks of the new government: they were required to have profound contents and a novelty, vivid, style that can attract people's attention. Meanwhile, the posters also catered to the international affairs, such as against the use of atomic bombs in 1955, and against British and American invasion into Iraq, Jordan and Lebanon in 1958.

In the 1960s China stopped following the artistic style of Soviet Union as it did in the 1950s, and many publicity posters of the Chinese style and spirit of the time appeared. Apart from the style, the themes were enriched: more works were created to reflect social welfare instead of sheer political contents.

Approaching the mid-1960s when the Cultural Revolution was about to come, political inclination in China was becoming more obvious than ever. Publicity campaigns of various titles followed one after another. During the 10-year Cultural Revolution, the unprecedented craze agitated mass criticism through publicity. In this period, all kinds of paintings were closely related to publicity, and thus the New China posters were pushed to peak in this fanatical political movements. At this time, the posters were characteristic of the use of bright red color, and the various dramatic poses of characters. Except for painters who were jailed for political incorrectness, countless posters were created by ordinary people during the Cultural Revolution. Posters were so commonly used that people even put them up on the walls as household decoration. It is fair to say that the 10 years of Cultural Revolution is an age of publicity posters.

The Decline

The Cultural Revolution was a destructive blow to China. The confusion of ideological ideas and severe poverty situations came along. People were tired of political movements as well as the publicity posters. From then on, the posters were drastically declining. Years later, they were hardly remembered by common people, and are often seen in the bookstalls for second-hand book collectors. Only some publishing houses can recall the past glory of this art. Except for the political hint of this art, the New China posters have been extruded by commercial ads which improved largely due to photography and digital processing technique. Nowadays, this art form is only used to commemorate political events, such as the returns of Hong Kong and Macao, and events concerning public welfare, such as prevention and treatment of AIDS. This art is still of obvious Chinese characteristics, but few cares to develop it any more.

L E A D E R S

1

1

1 Marching Under the Banner of Mao Zedong / Zhang Ding / 1949

2

2 Chairman Mao Leads Us to Build Great Homeland / Li Qi / 1953

3

3 To Love the Communist Party and Chairman Mao / Li Mubai / 1958

4

4 The Communiqué on the Greeting of Mao Zedong and Nikita Khrushchev / Sha Gengshi / 1958

5

5 To Strive to Build up Our Nation as a Great Socialist Country as Soon as Possible / Tian Yuwen / 1958

6

6 Our Victory Is the Victory of Marxism-Leninism in China / Jin Shangyi / 1961

7

8

7 All the People Follow the Same Cause, led by the Communist Party / Chen Huiming / 1962
8 To Commemorate the 25th Anniversary of the Launch of the "Talks at the Yan'an Forum on Literature and Art", the Great Writing of Chairman Mao / Anonymous / 1967

9

9 To Celebrate the 18th Anniversary of the Founding of the Peoples' Republic of China / Anonymous / 1967

10

10 Following the "May 7th Instruction" of Chairman Mao, Marching towards Our Bright Future / Anonymous / During the 1960s

11

11 We Will Make man-made satellites Too / Anonymous / 1970

12

12 Watching the waves of Rice and Bean Fields happily, with efficient workers mavching at dusk / Anonymous / 1970

13

13 Long live the great, glorious, and correct Communist Party of China / Anonymous / 1971

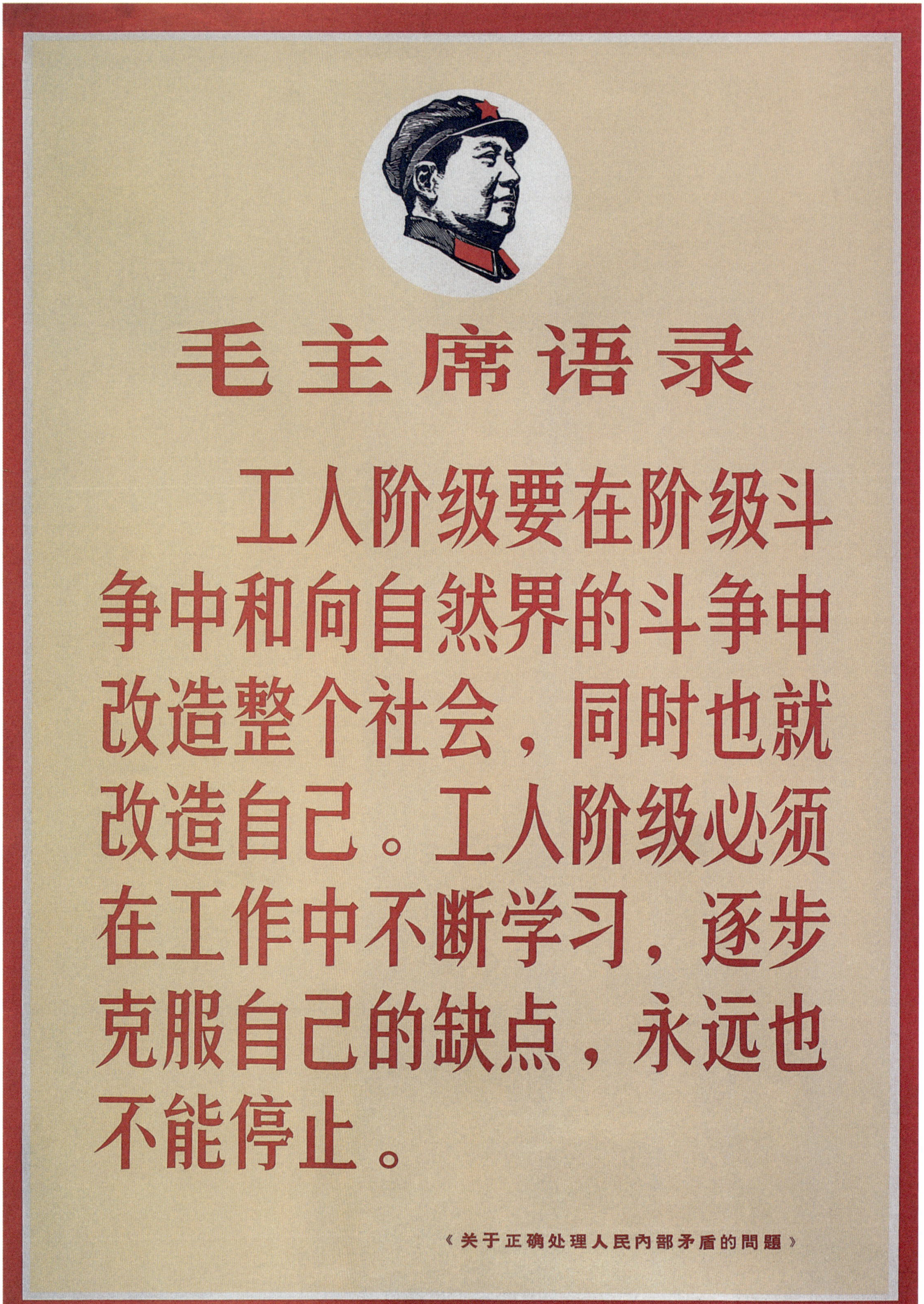

14

14 Quotations from Chairman Mao / Anonymous / Dateless

15

15 Commemorate the 30th Anniversary of the Launch of the "Talks at the Yan'an Forum on Literature and Art", the Great Writing of Chairman Mao / Gu Yuan, Zhan Jianjun / 1972

16

16 To Chairman Mao in Counter-Japanese Military and Political University / Liu Wenxi / 1978

17

18

17 Chairman Mao Is the Greatest Contemporary Marxist / Tang Xiaohe / 1976
18 Contributing to Accelerate the Realization of the Four Modernizations / Tan Difu / 1979

P O L I T I C S

2

19

19 To Firmly Advocate the Statement of Premier Zhou / Central Institute of Arts and Crafts / 1958

20

20 We Are the Guards and the Constructors of the Socialist Cause / Central Institute of Arts and Crafts / 1958

21

21 The Torrent of Communism Crashes All the Hard Stone / Central Institute of Arts and Crafts / 1958

22

22 Communism Is Thriving, While Capitalism Is Heading towards a Dead End / Department of Arts and Crafts from Xi 'an Academy of Fine Arts / 1958

23

24

23 To Go in for the People's Commune / Xiao Lin / 1958
24 The Garden of Literature and Art Is Filled with the Flower Fragrances; To Sing to Celebrate the Founding of Our Country Together / Wang Jiao / 1959

25

26

25 China Is Capable of Defeating the Invaders / Zhang Ruji / 1958
26 To Be a Jack-of-all-trades in Agricultural Production / Huang Jing / Dateless

27 Long Live the People's Republic of China / Sha Gengshi / 1959

27

28

28 Wish the People's Heroes Eternal Lives / Arts and Crafts Department of the Luxun Academy of Fine Arts / 1959

29

29 Celebrating the 10th Anniversary of Victory / Arts and Crafts Department of the Luxun Academy of Fine Arts / 1959

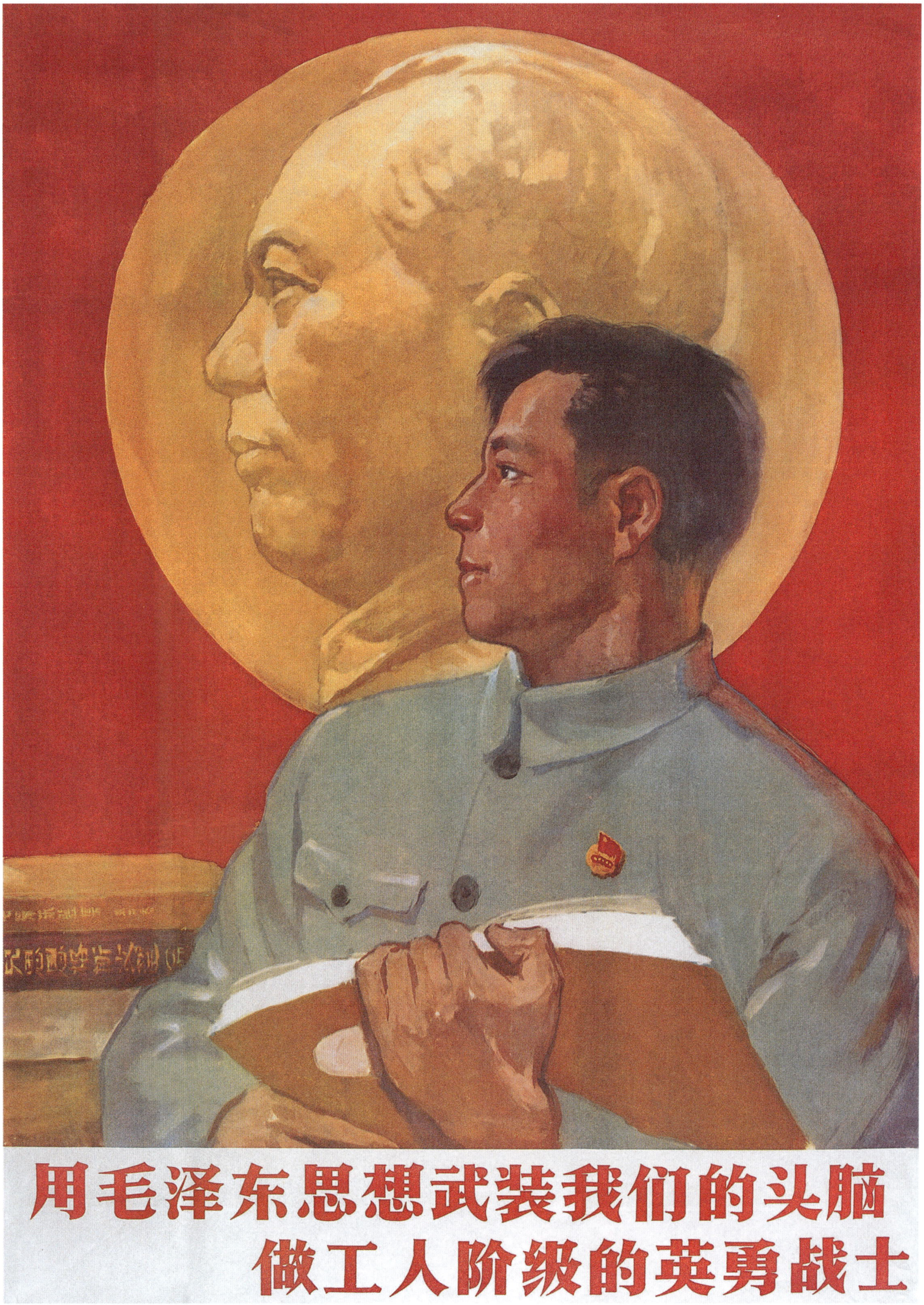

30

30 To Arm Our Brains with Maoism, and Be the Brave Warriors of the Working Class / Zhou Guangjie / 1960

31

31 To Let the Advanced Ideas Flourish Everywhere / Shen Yi and more / Dateless

32

32 Long Live the People's Commune / Yang Huangzhao / 1960

33

33 To March Onward Victoriously Under the Banner of Mao Zedong / Huang Chuanwei, Sun Nengzi / 1962

34

34 The Deeper the Soil We Plough, The Higher the Satellites We Launch / Huang Jing / Dateless

35

35 The Communist Party Is the Red Sun of the Chinese People / Jiang Nanchun / 1964

36

37

36 To Arm Ourselves with Maoism, and Be the Firm Successors of Revolution / Zhang Yanling / 1965

37 To Boost Revolution, Increase Production, and Support the Patriotic Compatriots in Hong Kong and Kowloon with the Anti-British Struggle / Anonymous / Dateless

38

38 Long Live the People's Republic of China / Zhang Ruji, Sheng Cijun, and Tian Yuwen / 1964

39

39 To Support the Army and Cherish the People / Anonymous / 1970

40

40 Long Live the Maoism / Anonymous / 1970

41 Long Live the Great, Honorable, and Righteous Communist Party of China / Anonymous / 1971

41

42

42 Learning from the Working Class / Liang Yan / 1972

43

43 Long Live the Great Communist Party of China / Jiang Nanchun, Yao Zhongyu / 1974

44

45

44 Going All the Way through by Combining the Two Forces of Workers and the Peasants / Wang Yang / 1974
45 Socialism Marches Onwards Victoriously in Every Way / Yu Zhenli / 1974

46

47

46 Band Together to Fight for Bigger Victory / Yan Yongsheng / 1974

47 Following the Revolutionary Line Raised by Chairman Mao with Courage and Energy / Ben She / 1974

48

49

48 Carrying out the Socialist Cause Initiated by Chairman Mao / Hebei Fine Arts Publishing House / 1976

49 Cheering the Triumphant Opening of the 4th National People's Congress, and Following the Revolutionary Route Raised by Chairman Mao with Courage and Energy / Wu Min / 1975

50

51

50 Carrying forward the Spirit of Solidarity and Militancy, and March Onwards to Victory / Ghazi Ahmed, Liu Nansheng, and Li Zhuo / 1975

51 Marching Onwards Victoriously, Following the Revolutionary Route Raised by Chairman Mao / Anonymous / Dateless

52

53

53 Swimming Forward against the Great Storms / The Coordinate Headquarter of the 10th Anniversary of Yangtze Swimming / Dateless

54

54 The Communist Party of China Is the Core Force that Leads Us towards Our Cause / Zhou Shuqiao / 1976

55

55 Long Live the Great, Honorable, and Righteous Communist Party of China / Li Zhiguo / 1977

56

57

56 Celebrating the Triumphant Opening of the Third Plenary Session of the 10th Central Committee of the CPC / The Cultural Center of the Xinjin county, Liaoning province / 1977

57 Cheering the Successful Opening of the 5th National People's Congress / An Yaohua / 1977

58

59

58 To Eat, Live and Work with Farmers, and Continue the Revolution / Wang Lizhi, Meng Jinyuan / 1977
59 To Smash the "Gang of four", and Promote the Peoples's Communes of Dazhai Town / Wu Di / 1977

60

60 Thousands of Armed Soldiers Sweep off the "Gang of four" / Shen Shaolun / 1976

61

61 To Completely Expose and Criticize the "Gang of four" / Sun Quan / 1977

62

63

63 The New Constitution: People's Aspiration / Zhou Ruizhuang / 1978

64

65

64 Giving Full Play to the Main Force of Working Class / Chao Deren / 1978

65 Hundreds of Flowers Is Blooming in Our Motherland / Zhang Yuliang / 1979

66 Upholding the Four Fundamental Principles, and Striving to Realize the Four Modernizations / Ma Jindong / 1981

065 | Politics

67

68

67 Long Live China / Huang Jiong / 1981
68 Always Following the Communist Party / Wang Yanlin / 1981
69 Our Flag Is Communism / Qiu Baiping / 1982

69

70

71

70 Long Live the People's Republic of China / Jia Hongxun / 1989
71 Long Live the Communist Party of China / Jia Hongxun / 1989
72 Celebrating the Return of Hong Kong to China Joyfully / Chen Jiahua / 1997

72

I N T E R N A T I O N A L

3

072 ~ 103

73

73 Welcome the Year 1951 / Wang Liuqiu / 1950

74

74 Celebrating the Successful Holding of the Asian and Pacific Peace Conferences / Sha Gengshi / 1952

75

75 We Ardently Love Peace / Yan Han / 1952

76

76 The Dear, Honorable People / Luo Gongliu / 1953

77

78

77 Fighting for Peace and Friendship, and Objecting to the Use of Atomic Weapons / Wang Juping / 1955
78 Long Live the United World Proletariats / Tian Yuwen / 1958

79

79 The Communique on the Greeting of Mao Zedong and Nikita Khrushchev / Li Hongren / 1958

80

81

80 Celebrating the Great International Workers' Day / Yuan Yunfu / 1958
81 Hurray for Peace and Friendship / Cao Jianfeng / 1959

82

82 Commemorating the 90th Birthday of the Great Leader of Revolution Vladimir Lenin / Jiang Zhaohe / 1960

83

83 Long Live the Sino-Soviet Friendship / Li Tianxiang, Zhao Youping / 1960

84

84 Celebrating the 10th Anniversary of the Signing of Sino-Soviet Treaty of Friendship, Alliance and Mutual Assistance / Yuan Yunfu / 1960

85

86

86 To Let the American Invaders Taste Our Steely Fists / Yang Wanfu / Dateless

87

87 Aiding Vietnam in the Anti-American War with Practical Actions / Anonymous / Dateless

88

88 To Burn the "God of Plague" / Central Institute of Arts and Crafts / 1960

89

89 The Realization of Worldwide Peace Requires People's Struggle / Sha Gengshi / 1960

90

90 Long Live the Sino-Soviet Friendship / Sha Gengshi / 1961

91

91 The USA Is Doomed to Fail, While Cuba Is Bound to Win / Zhang Ruji / 1962
92 In Support of the Righteous Opposition of Cubans Against the American Imperialism / Sha Gengshi / 1962
93 The Sovereignty of Cuba Must Not Be Violated / Wang Jiao / 1962

反对美帝国主义侵略古巴!美国必败!古巴必胜!
支持古巴政府的五项正义主张
保卫古巴!
保卫古巴革命!
古巴必胜!
向英雄的古巴人民致敬!
支持古巴人民反对美帝国主义的正义斗争!

92

古巴主权决不允許侵犯!

93

94

94 To Get the American Imperialism out of Congo / Zhang Wenxin / 1964

95

95 Oriving the Colonialists and Neo-colonialists out of Africa / Wang Datong, Du Yongqiao / 1964

96

96 The Victory Must Belong to the Dominican People / Dong Chensheng / 1965

97

97 To Get out of Dominica, American Imperialism! / Cao Zhenfeng / 1965

98

98 Strongly Objecting to American Imperialist Armed Invasion of the Democratic Republic of Vietnam / Zhang Yanling / 1964

99

99 American Imperialism Will Certainly Fail, While People All around the World Are Bound to Win / Anonymous / 1970

100 People all over the World Are United to Fight against the American Invaders and Their Followers
/ Civil Air Defence Office of Sichun Province / 1970

100

101

101 Proletarians all over the World Are United Together / PLA Pictorial / 1971

102

102 International Communism Must Be Realized / Creative Team of the Beijing Fine Arts Company / Dateless

103

103 Giving a Warm Welcome to Our Asian and African Friends / The Revolutionary Committee of the Beijing Stamp Factory / 1971

104

104 Long Live the Friendship of Athletes between China and the Other Countries in the World / Shen Yaoyi / 1976

105

106

106 The Flower of Friendship Is Flourishing / Xu Chengzhi / 1983

MILITARY AFFAIRS AND NATIONAL DEFENSE

4

106 ~ 125

107

107 We Must Liberate Taiwan! / Hu Tuozhong, Ma Ding / 1954

108

108 Long Live the Chinese People's Liberation Army / Yuan Yunfu, Qian Yuehua / 1956

109

109 Turning Every Man into a Soldier to Protect Our Peace / Tan Yunsen / 1958

110

110 Reinforcing the Proletarian Dictatorship and the International Unity of Proletarians / Central Institute of Arts and Crafts / 1958

111

112

111 To Reinforce the War Preparedness to Defend Our Coasts / PLA Pictorial / 1962

112 To Improve Fighting Skills to Protect Our Homeland / PLA Pictorial / 1962

113 To be on the Alert to Guard Our Airspace / PLA Pictorial / 1962

113

114

114 Iron Bastion: Joint Defence by the Army and the People / Anonymous / Dateless

115

115 Learning and Practising When Available / Hua Kexiong / 1964

116

117

116 As Bold as Tiger on Land, and as Adept in Water as Flood Dragon / Anonymous / 1965
117 Being Valorous to Kill the Enemies, and Making the Bayonet Bleed / Anonymous / Dateless
118 Throwing the Grenade to Fight the Enemies, and Making Them Explode Like a Blooming Flower / Anonymous / 1965

刀見紅
害的队伍，部队政治质量
敢的标志是刺刀见红。

狠投猛打 敌群开花
在短兵相接时主要是用手榴弹，它是重要的
近战武器，不仅要投得远，同时还要投得准。

118

119

120

119 Tactful, Bold, and Unbeatable / Anonymous / Dateless
120 Destroying the Enemies and Defending Our Army / Anonymous / Dateless
121 With Hatred towards the Enemies in Mind, Not a Single Shot Will Miss Its Target / Anonymous / Dateless

保存自己
一方面要减少自己损
完成各种射击散兵坑。

胸怀仇恨 弹无虚发
特别要抓紧学射击，战斗中间最大量最普遍的硬本事就是射击。一定要把射击训练搞好。

121

122

123

122 Be It Daytime or Nighttime, Be It from the Upper Air or Low Altitude, We Will Destroy All the Hostile Planes / Ren Weixin / 1965

123 Be on the Alert to Protect Our Homeland and Destroy All the Invaders / Fine Arts Department of the Nanjing Normal University / 1969

124

125

124 Even with the Last Breath, We Will Destroy as Many Enemies as We Could / Fine Arts Team of the Military Museum of the Chinese People's Revolution / 1970

125 Being Ready to Destroy the Enemies Anytime / Xie Linghu, Qin Tianjian / 1970

126

126 Being on the Alert to Protect Our Homeland / The Revolutionary Committee of the No.9 Qingdao National Cotton Factory / 1972

127

127 The American Atomic Bomb Is Just a Paper Tiger / Civil Air Defence Office of Liaoning Province / 1972

128

128 The People's War Thought Raised by Chairman Mao Will Shine Forever / The Political Department of the 81544 Unit / 1977

129

129 The People's Army That Creates, Leads and Commands / Wu Min / 1977

130

131

131 Learning from the 8th Company of the Chinese People's Liberation Army Stationed in the Nanjing Road / You Longgu / 1992

ECONOMIC DEVELOPMENT

5

128 ~ 175

132

132 Joining the Rural Credit Cooperative Is the Way to Common Prosperity / Zhang Fanfu, Wu Dezu, and Zhaoyu / 1945

133

133 To Make the Crops Grow Well, One must Often Carry the Manure Basket; The More Manure We Accumulate in Spring, the More Harvest We get in Autumn / Anonymous / Dateless

134

135

135 Learning the Advanced Experience from the Soviet Union, Giving Full Play to Your Wisdom and Strength, and Accomplish Bigger Ambitions / Jin Shangyi, Fu Zhigui / 1954

136

136 Increasing the Production of Oil Plants to Satisfy Our Country's Need / Yang Xianrang / 1954

137

138

137 We Are a New and Fresh Team of Our Homeland's Peaceful Construction / Feng Fasi / 1954
138 Caring for the Machines the Way We Cherish Our Eyes / Zhang Ruji / 1955

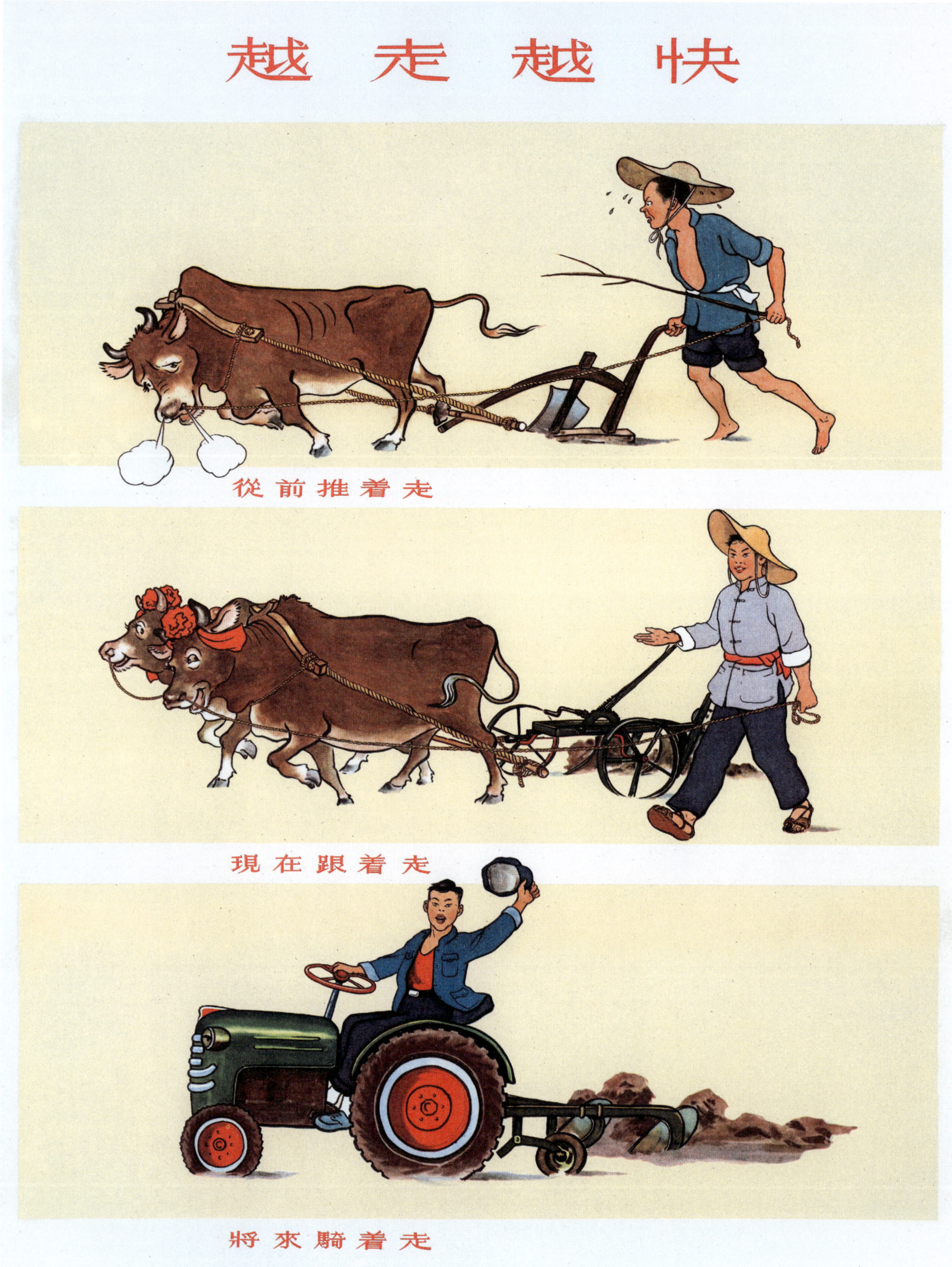

139

139 To Go Faster and Faster / Lian Wen / 1956

140

140 The Crops Look Healthily Golden, Which Suggests the Cooperative Production Mode Is Workable / Lin Kai / 1956

141

141 We Turn Our Hatred towards the Enemies into the Strong Enthusiasm towards Improving Domestic Production / Zhang Ruji / 1958

142

142 Revolutionizing the Farm Implements, and Taking a Great Leap Forward in Production / Zhang Wenxin / 1958

143

143 Organizing Canteens of the People's Commune Well / Anonymous / Dateless

144

144 Inviting Everyone to Eat Some Sweet Potatoes / Sha Gengshi / 1958

145

146

146 Taking Advantage of the Water Conservancy by Digging Wells and Channeling; Striving for an Extensive Agricultural Harvest / Jin Zhilin / 1958

147 Applying the Marxism-Leninism to Practical Work / Su Tianci / 1958

148

148 Producing More Steel and Beating up the American Wolves / Wu Fanxiang / 1958

149

149 John Rides Bull and I Ride Horse; It Is a Joke If I Lose / Xu Qixiong / 1958

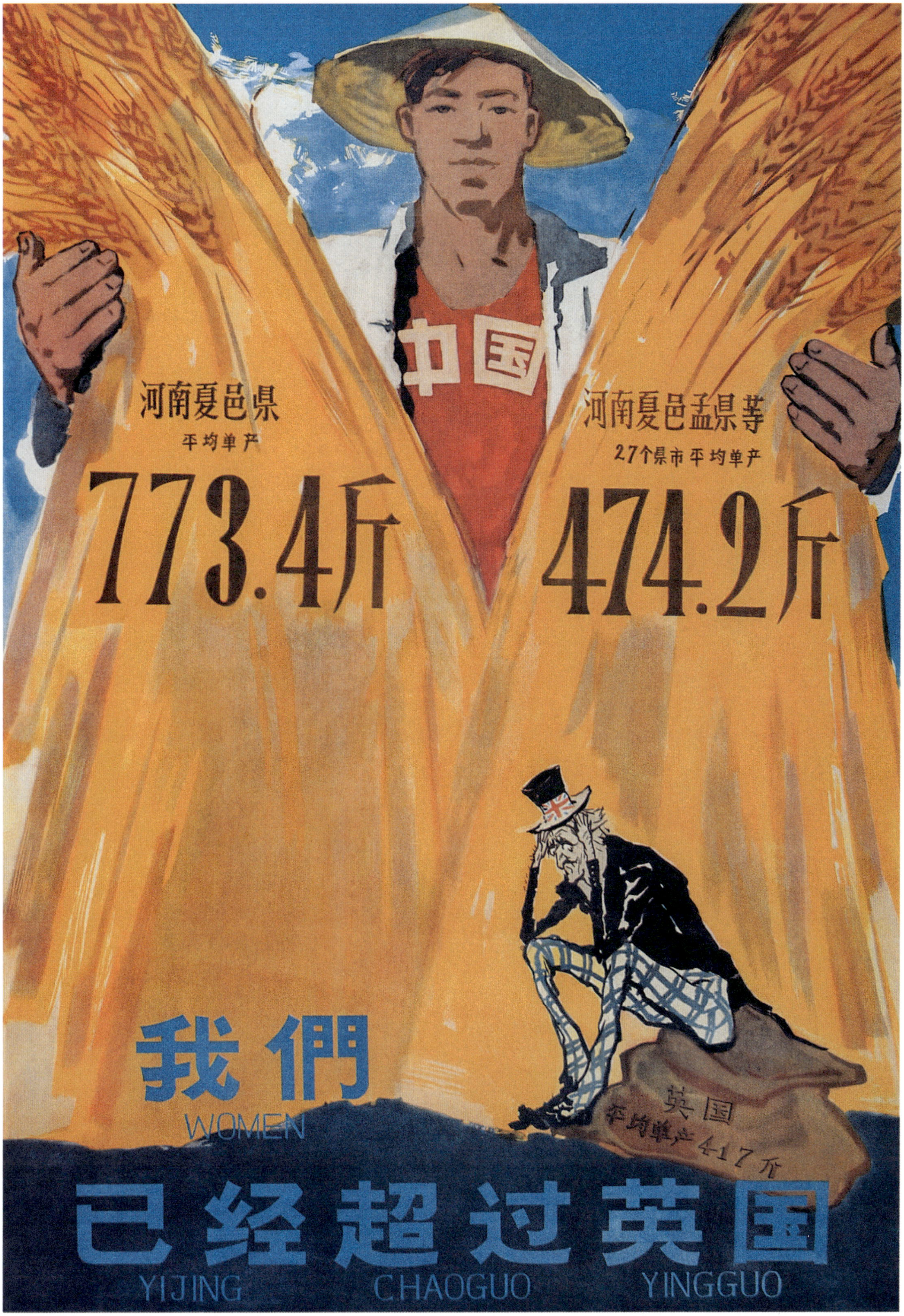

150

150 We Have Surpassed the Britain / Luo Er'chun, Ping Ye / 1958

151 Comrades, We Must Ensure Safety Production / Zhang Yuhai / Dateless

152

152 Listening to the Party / Lin Tao / 1960

153

153 Ensuring the Harvest of Grains and the Large Production of Steel / Huang Jing / 1961

154

154 The Fragrance of Rice Is Spread for Miles, and Everybody Is Showing Its Reaping Technique / Sheng Cijun / 1961

155

155 If We Choose the Good-Quality Seeds to Plant, We Can Increase the Production Every Year / Jin Meisheng / 1964

156

156 Learning the Working Ethos from Dazhai Town, and Following Their Successful Way of Operating Agriculture / Yin Rongsheng / 1965

157

158

157 Striving to Accomplish the Agricultural Mechanization / The Revolutionary Committee of the Beijing No.76 Middle School / 1966

158 Holding Up High the Flag of Maoism, and Fighting for the Realization of the 3rd Five-Year Plan / Zhang Ruji, Fei Shengfu / 1966

159

159 To Enforce the Social Revolution, We Dare to Surpass the Advanced World Levels / Qian Daxin / 1966

160

160 All the People Work Together and Be the Heroes that Are Good at Forging Iron / Chen Zhong / 1968

161

161 Saving Everything for the Revolution / The Revolutionary Committees of the Shanghai Valve Factory No.1 and the Shanghai Siping Road No.2 Primary School / 1970

162 Reforming the Land of China with Determination and Courage / The Pictorial of Linfen Workers, Peasants and Soldiers / 1971

改造中国
敢教襄汾换新天
为革命打井
老愚公战斗队
民兵连
人民公社好
战无不胜的毛泽东
思想万岁！
最高指示
水利是农
业的命脉。
水利建设
指挥部
水利机具展览会
沿着毛主席革命路线胜利前进！
自力更生
艰苦奋斗
活学活用
毛主席哲学著作
讲用会
阶级教育展览
大力支援农业建设
青年突击队
毛泽东思想
宣传队
支农服务队
民兵连
农业学大寨
抗旱大军

162

163

164

163 There Is No Obstacle That We Cannot Overcome For the Cause of Revolution / Anonymous / 1970

164 Striving to Accomplish the 4th Five-Year Plan of Constructing Our National Economy / The Revolutionary Committee of the Construction Brigade of the Xuhui District Building Company / 1971

165

166

165 Upholding Comprehensive Utilization to Create More Wealth for Our Motherland / The Amateur Artistic Creation Team of the Beijing General Brewery / 1971

166 Developing the Industries of the People's Communes in the County, So as to Serve the Development of Agriculture / Creative Team of the Hebei People's Publishing House / 1971

167

168

167 Learning from Daqing in Industry / The Information Office of the Political and Ideological Team of the Guangzhou Revolutionary Committee / 1971

168 Developing Agriculture by Learning from Dazhai Town / The Locomotive Depot of the Railway of Bei'an, Heilongjiang / 1971

169

170

169 Striving to Reverse the Transportation of Coal from the North to the South of China / Yi Fasheng, Wu Chenlei / 1972

170 Developing Coal Fields in the Jiangnan region, and Rapidly Reverse the Transportation of Coal from the North to the South of China / The Artistic Creation Classes for Changzhou Workers, Peasants and Soldiers / 1972

171

172

172 Developing Scientific Agriculture to Produce High-Yield Grains and Cottons / Zhang Yichun, Liu Zhongfu, and Shen Tongjing / 1973

173

174

175

174 Contributing More to Agricultural Mechanization / The Artistic Team of the Publicity Department of the Guangzhou Municipal Committee / 1973

175 Accelerating the Pace of Agricultural Mechanization, and Fight for the Modernization of Agriculture / Liu Wenxi / 1975

176

176 Women Hold Up Half the Sky, Which Refreshes the Image of Our Country / Wang Dawei / 1975

177

177 Learning from Daqing in Industry / Yang Keshan / 1976

178

178 Digging Wells for Better, Faster and More Economical Achievements / Creative Team of the Hebei People's Publishing House / Dateless

179

179 Making More and Better Steel for Our Motherland / Zhong Zhihong / 1976

180

181

180 Developing Industry with the Aim of Increasing Steel Production / Feng Jianqin, Chen Dexi / 1976
181 Uniting to Fight, and We Are Sure to Win over Nature / Hebei Fine Arts Publishing House / 1976

182

183

182 Workers and Peasants Join Hands / Guangzhou Fine Arts Team / 1977

183 The Fundamental Way out for Agriculture Lies in Mechanization / Zhang Wen / 1977

184

184 A Warm Welcome to the Conventioneers of the Meeting of Learning from Daqing in Industry / Zhang Ruji, Wang Jiao / 1977

185

185 Developing Socialism Is Reasonable, Meritorious, and Honorable / Xu Xi / 1977

186

187

186 Working Hard and Sweating Through Shirt to Contribute More to Socialism / Yang Keshan / 1978
187 Fighting for Basically Realizing Agricultural Mechanization in 1980 / Liu Wenxi / 1980

188

189

188 Keeping Up Our Spirits to Fight for Vitalizing Hebei Province / An Yaohua / 1983
189 Keeping in Mind the Spirit of Solidarity and Strive to Revitalize China / Hao Yang / 1983

NATIONAL UNITY

6

178 ~ 189

190

191

190 Uniting 56 Ethnic Groups, and Living Happily Ever After / Huang Zhou / 1959
191 All the Ethnic Groups Are Closely United to Build Our Strong, Flourishing Homeland / Weng Yizhi / 1963

192

192 Long Live the Communist Party of China / Zhang Ruji, Sheng Cijun, and Tian Yuwen / 1964

哪怕雀兒山高連天，
哪怕大渡河深万丈，
把公路修向拉薩，
把幸福帶給西藏。
編劇
王冰
徐怀中
高平
导演
胡奇
V·息斯
李俊
总摄影师
J·伐湼希
通向拉萨的
幸福道路

193

194

194 Today's Tibet / Anonymous / Dateless

195 United to Fight for a Bigger Victory / Ha Qiongwen / 1974

195

196

196 Long Live the Communist Party of China / Wang Weishu, Shen Shaolun / 1974

197

198

197 All the Ethnic Groups Sing Loudly the Song "The East Is Red" / Fu Qizhong / 1974
198 Athletes from Different Ethnic Groups Are United and Looking Forward to the Bright Future / Shen Yaoyi, Shen Yaoding / 1975

199 Uniting All the Ethnic Groups, and Living Happily Ever After / Gao Quan, Yang Keshan / 1979

199

200

200 Warmly Hailing the Region-Wide Nadam Fair of the Inner Mongolia Autonomous Region / Anonymous / 1982

201

201 People from All Ethnic Groups Take Part in the Population Census / Chen Zhenxin / 1982

CULTURE AND EDUCATION

7

202

202 Women Hold Up Half the Sky, and Compete with Men in Every Way: They Are Excellent in Production and Trooping Training / Liu Peiwu / Dateless

203

203 Women and Men of the People's Republic of China Share Equal Rights in Politics, Economy, Culture, Society and Household / Hong Bo, Wu Biduan / 1954

204

204 Building Up an Army of Thousands of Working-Class Intellectuals / Central Institute of Arts and Crafts / 1956

205 Devoting the Youth to Our Motherland, and Creating Our Happy Future / Chen Yunhe / 1957

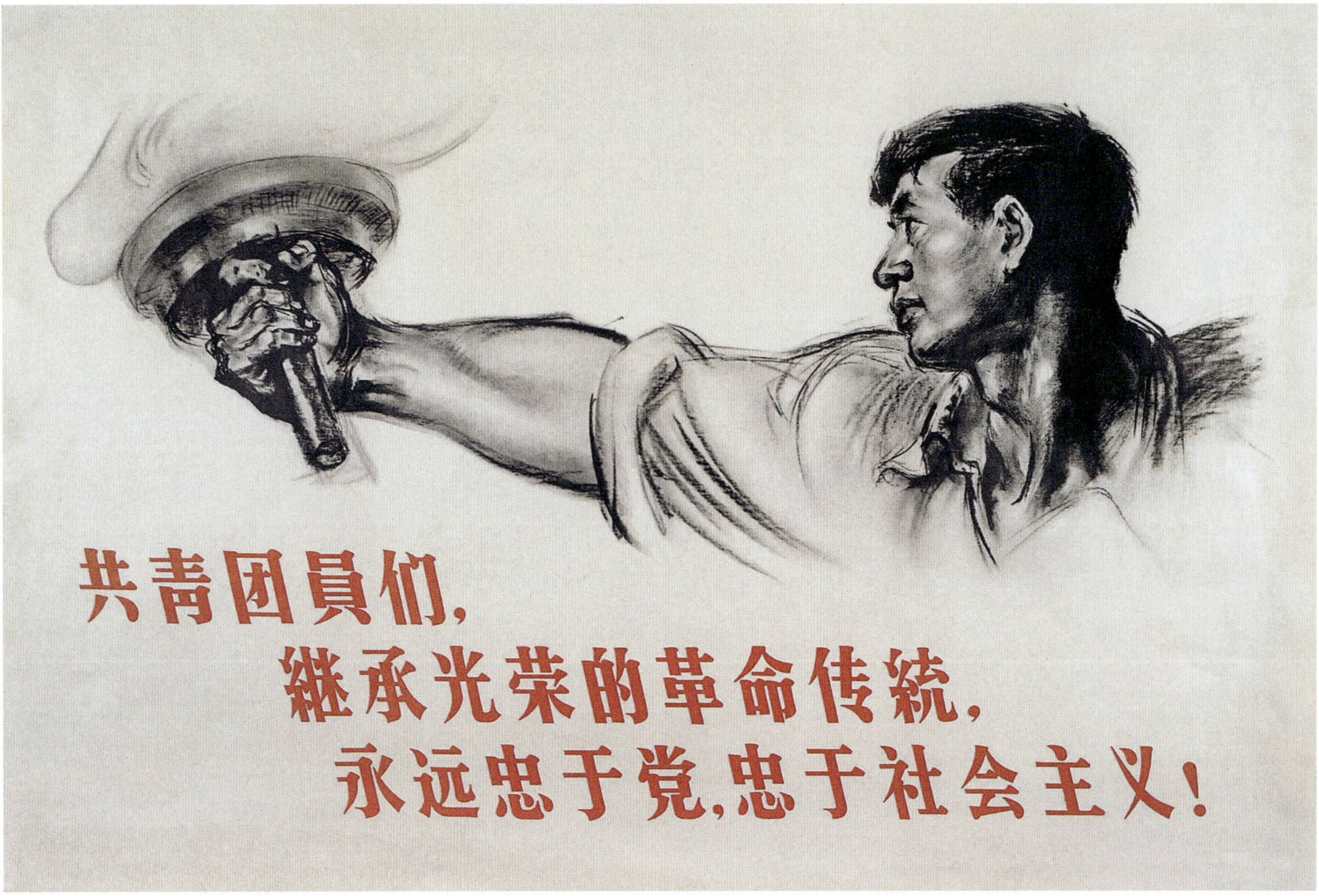

206

207

206 Members of the Communist Youth League Inherit Honorable Traditions of Chinese Revolution; They Vow to Devote Themselves to the Communist Party and Socialism / Qiu Sha / 1957

207 The Youth Is Like a Rising Sun: We Pin Our Hopes on You / Zhan Jianjun / 1958

208

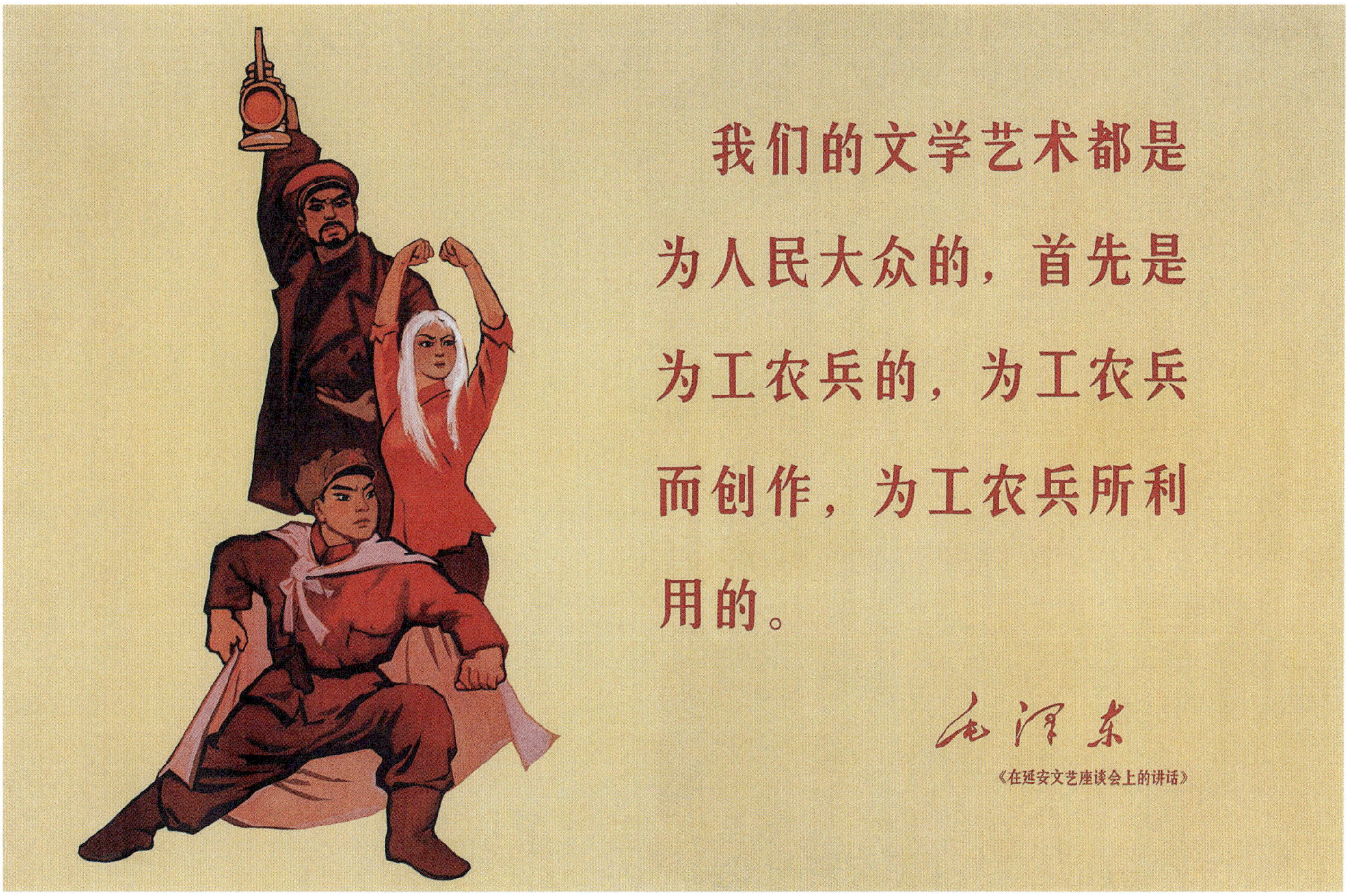

209

208 Learning Aerial Knowledge, and Preparing to Serve Our Motherland / Shao Jingkun / 1958

209 Talks at the Yan'an Forum on Literature and Art / Jingangshan Commune of the Beijing Film Academy / Dateless

210

210 Mastering Cultural and Scientific Knowledge to Serve Production Better / Cao Youcheng / 1959

211

211 Welcome the First National Sports Meeting / Preparatory Committee of the First National Sports Meeting of the People's Republic of China / 1959

212

212 We Will Become Real-plane Pilots in the Future / Chen Qing / Dateless

213

213 We Are Ship Model Lovers Today, But We Will Become Pioneers of Ship Makers in the Future / Deng Zhiying, Jin Guiquan / 1960

214

214 Arming Ourselves with Maoism, and Climbing Over the Peak of Culture and Science / Liu Yongkai / 1960

215

215 With Firm Resolve to Succeed, We Will Climb Over the Peak of Culture and Science / Ge Weimo / 1962

216

216 Inheriting the Honorable Tradition of Children's Corps, and Becoming the Successors of Communism / Qin Dahu, Wang Yufang / 1965

217

217 Promising Youth Grows Strong in Every Field / The Artistic Team of the Publicity Department of the Guangzhou Municipal Committee / 1973

218

218 Mastering Scientific and Cultural Knowledge / Li Gengchen / Dateless

219

219 Passionately Carrying out Mass Sports Activities / Liao Yiqun / 1974

220

220 Inheriting the Sharp Insights into Social Reality, and Pass It on to the Next Generation / Xiao Zhenya, Liu Sibin / 1975

221

221 Learning from Lu Xun's Revolutionary Spirit / Wang Huaiqing / 1976

222

222 Build Up Our Body, We Be the Successors of Chinese Revolution
When We Grow Up / Guangzhou Fine Arts Studio / 1975

223

223 Passionately Joining in Sports Activities, and Work out for Revolution / Guangzhou Fine Arts Studio / 1975

224

225

224 Marching on Victoriously Following the Revolutionary Line on Literature and Art Raised by Chairman Mao / Shen Yaoyi / 1975

225 The Friendship Invitational Tournament of the Shanghai International Table Tennis Held in 1976 / Anonymous / 1976

226

227

226 Implementing the Birth Control Policy for Revolution / Zhang Baogui / Dateless

227 The Birth Control Policy Has Many Advantages / Linfen County Cultural Center / Dateless

228

229

228 Creating Excellent Records to Win Glory for Our Motherland / Hu Zhenyu / 1978
229 Studying and Training Hard, Fighting to Surpass World Advanced Levels / An Yaohua / 1978

230

230 Passionately Carrying out Mass Sports Activities / Chen Chengqi / 1978

231

231 Study Hard and Improve Everyday / Guan Mansheng / 1978

232

232 Studying Hard and Improving Everyday / Lou Puyi, Zhang Youlong, and Ganshu Province Education Conference / 1978

233

233 Listening Carefully in the Culture Class / Qi Chuanyu / 1978

234

234 We Are the Master of Science / Liao Yuyi, Ou Huanzhang / 1978

235

236

235 Becoming New Socialists who Fully Develop Morality, Intelligence, Physique and Aesthetics / Liu Changshun / 1978

236 Building up a New Relationship of Teachers and Students Based on Mutual Respect and Admiration / Wang Jinxiang / 1978

237

237 The Glory Belongs to People's Teachers / Wang Shenyi / 1978

238 Building Up Our Body / Chen Chengqi / 1979

239

239 We Love Science When We Are Young / He Bing / 1979

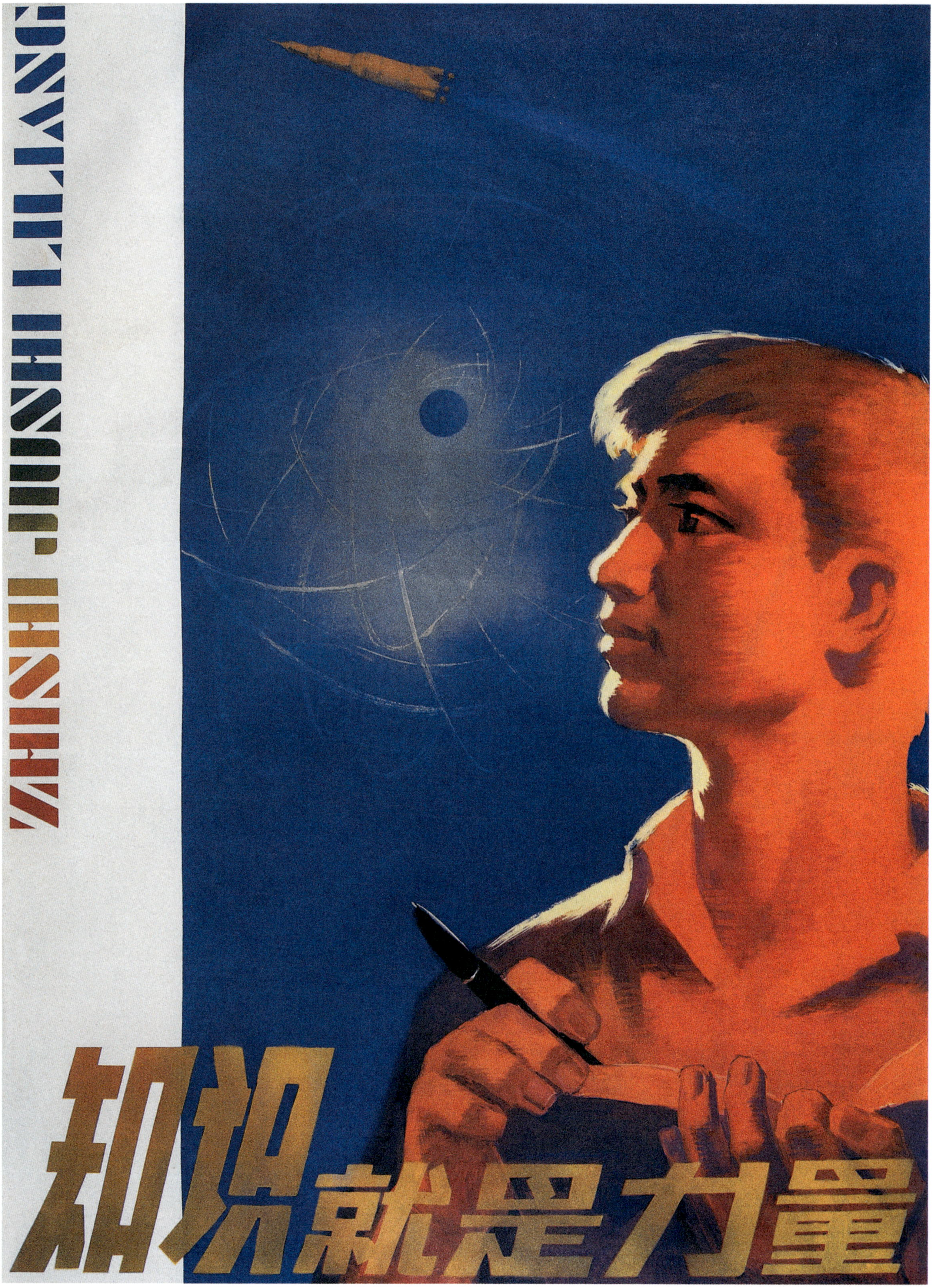

240

240 Knowledge Is Power / Zhang Zuying / 1979

241

241 Learning from Our Comrade Lei Feng / Li Mubai / 1979

242

242 Learning from Lei Feng, and Establishing a New Social Ethos / An Yaohua / 1979

243

243 Learning the Attitude of Caring for People in Every Way from Lei Feng / Jin Jifa / 1981

244

244 Love Our Country, Our People, and Our Communist Party; Studying Hard and Improving Everyday / Chao Deren / 1982

245 Leading a Thrifty Life, Paying Attention to Personal Hygiene, Do not Smoke, Drink, and Spit / Fu Zhisheng / 1982

246 Listening Carefully, Thinking Diligently, and Finishing Homework Earnestly / Yu Zhenli / 1982

245

246

247

247 Reporting Accurately the Number of Family Members to Help with the Population Census
/ Qiu Baiping, Leading Group Office of the Third Population Census of the State Council / 1982

248

248 Mobilizing All the People and Every Member of the Party / Cui Senlin / 1982

249

249 Devoting Our Youth and Wisdom to the Realization of the Four Modernizations / Chen Chengqi / 1983

250

250 Learning from Zhang Haidi: To Become the New Generation Youth with Morality, Ideal, Cultural Knowledge and Discipline / Qiu Baiping / 1983

251

251 Greeting Guests with Courtesy, Warmth and Thoughtfulness, and Operating Businesses with Integrity / Mao Wenbiao / 1983

252

252 Everybody Complies the Social Order, and Pays Attention to Social Morality / Wu Min / 1983

253

253 The Official Date of the National Sample Survey on the Status of Disabilities / Chao Deren / 1987

254

254 Lei Feng and His Red Scarf / Xu Fugen / 1988

255

255 Mobilizing Society at Large to Conduct the Fourth National Population Census / Chen Zhenxin / 1989

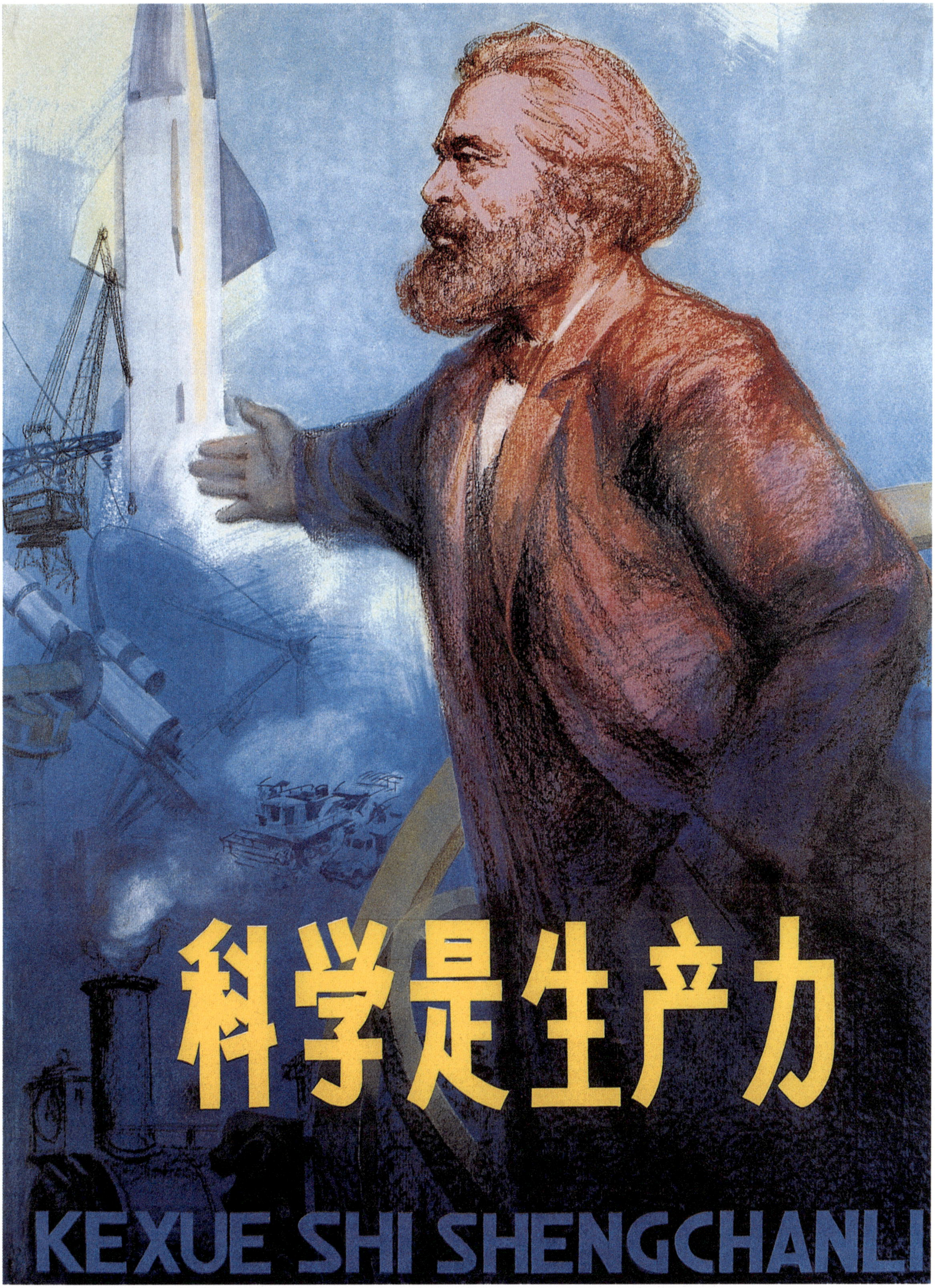

256

256 Science Is Productivity / Wen Guozhang / 1989

ACKNOWLEDGEMENTS

We would like to thank all the designers and contributors who have been involved in the production of this book; their contributions have been indispensable to its creation. We would also like to express our gratitude to all the producers for their invaluable opinions and assistance throughout this project. And to the many others whose names are not credited but have made helpful suggestions, we thank you for your continuous support.

FUTURE PARTNERSHIPS

If you wish to participate in SendPoints' future projects and publications, please send your website or portfolio to editor01@sendpoints.cn.